Origins

Battle of the Monster X-bot

Chris Priestley ✖ **Jonatronix**

OXFORD
UNIVERSITY PRESS

Previously …

In the story *Robot Rampage*, Max, Cat, Ant and Tiger go to see the opening of the new Robo-Rex II film – in 3D.

But, halfway through the film, a monster X-bot bursts through the screen, into the cinema. Dr X has sent the X-bot after the children … he wants their special watches.

The four friends make a run for it. The X-bot traps them in an alley. Then, Tiger has an idea. With the help of Ant, he grows his Robo-Rex II toy and battles the monster X-bot.

Robo-Rex is defeated. The X-bot grabs Cat and heads towards the NICE building. The three boys watch in horror as the X-bot starts to climb up the building. Will they be able to stop it and save their friend? Read on to find out ...

Max, Ant and Tiger watched in horror as the monster X-bot climbed higher and higher up the outside of the NICE building. They could hear its huge metal joints creaking as it climbed.

The X-bot grasped the building with its metal feet and used the window ledges for footholds. It looked like a hideous black insect silhouetted against the sky.

"Look!" gasped Ant, as the dome at the top of the building opened up. A large, metal tube rose out of the roof towards the dome. "It's heading for that. It must be a way into NICE ... and NASTI – the headquarters of Dr X," he gulped.

"Well, it can hardly fit through the front door, can it?" snapped Tiger. "But what are we going to do?"

"I don't know," said Ant, with a worried frown.

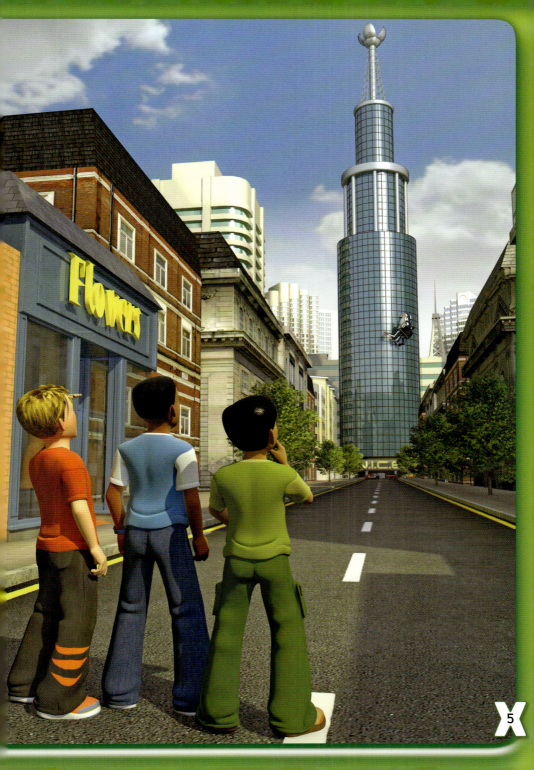

The boys could hardly see Cat at all now, she was so high up. Max looked around. The street was deserted. Most people in the city were at the bank holiday carnival on the other side of town, and those who had seen the X-bot in the cinema had run away as soon as it had appeared. Max knew it was up to them to save Cat.

The X-bot turned its enormous head to look down at them. Its red eyes glowed triumphantly.

"I hate that thing!" said Tiger, scowling. "Robo-Rex was our only hope!" He looked behind him to where his giant toy was lying, defeated in the road.

"We'll fix him, Tiger," said Max.

"But not in time to save Cat!" said Tiger. "Dr X has beaten us for sure this time. He'll get Cat's watch and then –"

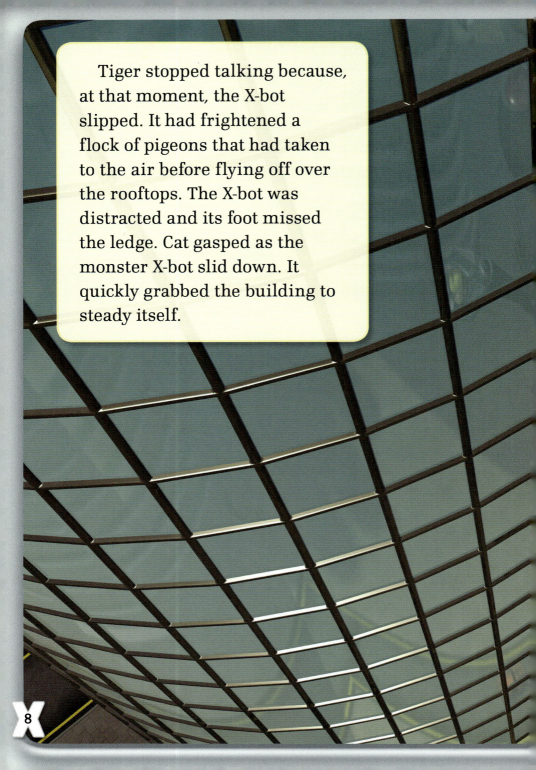

Tiger stopped talking because, at that moment, the X-bot slipped. It had frightened a flock of pigeons that had taken to the air before flying off over the rooftops. The X-bot was distracted and its foot missed the ledge. Cat gasped as the monster X-bot slid down. It quickly grabbed the building to steady itself.

Tiger's eyes grew wide with fear as he watched. "We have to get up there."

"But how?" cried Ant. "We'd need some sort of Robo-Bird!"

Max looked up at the X-bot and then across the road to a toyshop. "Maybe not," he said. "I've got an idea."

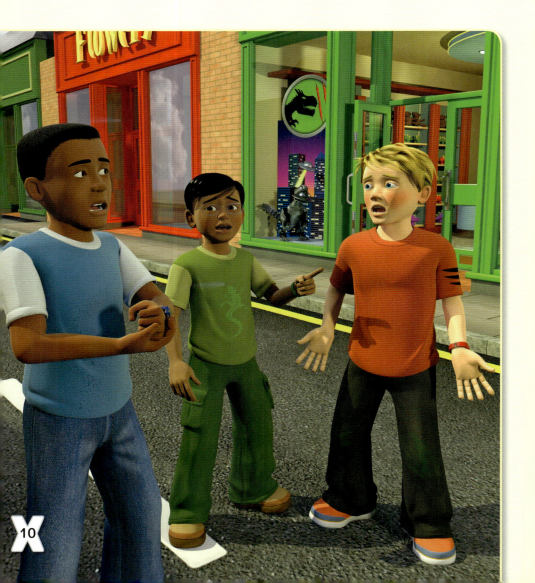

Chapter 2 - Max's idea

Ant and Tiger were baffled to see Max run over to the toyshop.

The man who worked there had run away with everyone else when the monster X-bot had first appeared. He had left the shop open.

Moments later, Max came back holding two toy planes.

"Genius!" said Tiger. "We can fly up there and rescue Cat!"

"You can't take those!" said Ant.

"I'm just borrowing them," said Max. "Besides, we don't really have time to argue, do we?"

They looked up. The X-bot was over halfway up the side of the building.

"You're right," said Ant. But he still looked uncomfortable.

Max guessed it was because Ant was afraid of heights. "Ant, you'll have to stay here. We need someone to help us take off ... it'll be quicker that way."

Ant looked relieved. "Well, if you insist," he said.

Tiger grabbed a plane. "I want this one!"

Max and Tiger put their planes on the ground.

Then they turned the dials on their watches.
They pushed the X and ...

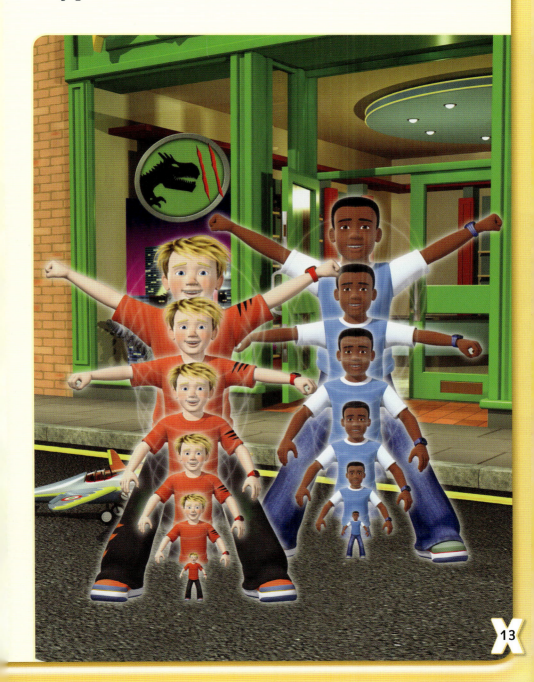

In an instant, Max and Tiger were micro-sized.

"Communication will be difficult up there," Max said to Tiger. "So take my lead."

"Yes, sir!" said Tiger, with a quick salute.

"The pigeons distracted the X-bot before," said Max, opening the door to the cockpit. "I'm hoping we can do the same thing. You watch out for Cat, OK?"

"Let's just go, shall we?" said Tiger.

The two boys quickly climbed into their planes and strapped themselves in.

Ant lifted up Max's plane first. He flicked the switch underneath it to turn the battery on. Then he spun the propeller at the front and the plane whirred into life. It shook in his hands as he pulled his arm back.

Then Ant jogged forwards a couple of steps and threw the plane into the air like a javelin.

"Arrggghhhh!" screamed Max, as he struggled to gain control of the plane.

He was heading straight towards the window of the toyshop. Max pulled back hard on the control column and, just as he was going to crash into the glass, the plane tilted up and began to climb.

"Sorry!" Ant called out.

Max banked the plane to the left and gave Ant an OK signal to say that he was all right.

It was Tiger's turn.

When Ant picked up Tiger's plane, he noticed that Tiger was looking a bit scared.

"Don't worry," said Ant, switching the plane on. "I've got the hang of it now!"

Tiger wasn't so sure.

Ant took a longer run up this time before he let Tiger's plane go. When he did, Tiger shot into the air even faster than Max.

Tiger's stomach lurched as he fought hard to steer the plane. He was already wondering if this was such a good idea. But then he looked up at the giant X-bot. It was getting near the top of the NICE building. He thought about Cat up there. He knew he had to carry on.

Max flew along beside him. They both pulled back on the controls and zoomed vertically upwards.

Cat looked down. The ground was getting further and further away. She was held firmly in the grip of the monster X-bot. But she was no longer terrified. She was angry. She had had enough of being carried about by some big, stupid robot. Cat tried again to pull her arm free.

"If only I could reach my watch ..." she said to herself. But it was no good. Her arms were clamped to her sides.

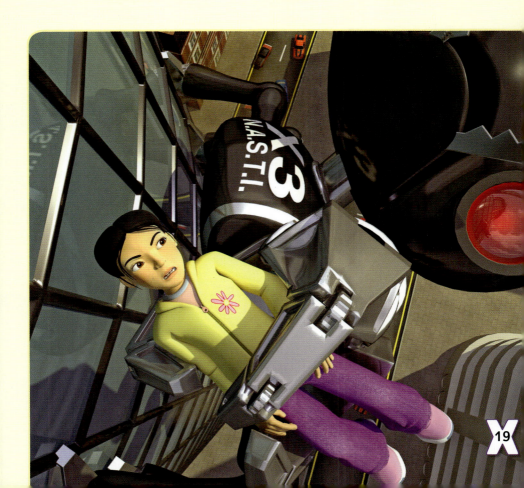

Then Cat heard a noise. Above the clunking and grinding of the X-bot's metal legs, she heard a whirring. It was faint at first but it grew louder and louder. Finally she saw the two planes. She had never been so relieved to see her friends in all her life.

As they flew up over the buildings, Max could make out the carnival in the distance. He thought about all the people there, having a good time and completely unaware of what was happening on the other side of the city. He felt a little envious of them.

Max focused on controlling the plane. It was not easy, as the plane was buffeted by the breeze. It felt more like he was driving over a bumpy road than flying through the air.

They were level with the X-bot now. Max gave Cat a quick wave. All she could do was smile back. Then Max pulled the control column to the right and flew directly towards the monster X-bot's head.

"Wait for me," shouted Tiger.

The X-bot saw them coming and gnashed its metal jaws. It reached out and swiped at the planes as if they were annoying flies. Max turned his plane sharply one way, Tiger went the other way. The X-bot seemed furious and tried to swipe at them both at the same time. It lost its grip on the building and began to slide ...

The noise of the X-bot's metal claws scraping against the building was deafening. It rang through Cat's head and made her teeth hurt. The X-bot scratched at the glass, trying to hold on, but it was no good. It needed all of its legs to hold on. It had to let Cat go.

Cat began to scream, paddling uselessly in the air as she fell.

Chapter 4 - Landing

As soon as Tiger saw the X-bot let go of Cat, he shoved the control column hard forwards and plunged into a vertical dive.

"Cat!" he yelled.

He had to save his friend. But the plane was much smaller than she was. There was no way it could take her weight, unless ...

"Turn the dial, Cat," he said to himself. "Turn the dial NOW!"

Cat reached for her watch and turned the dial.
She pressed the X and ...

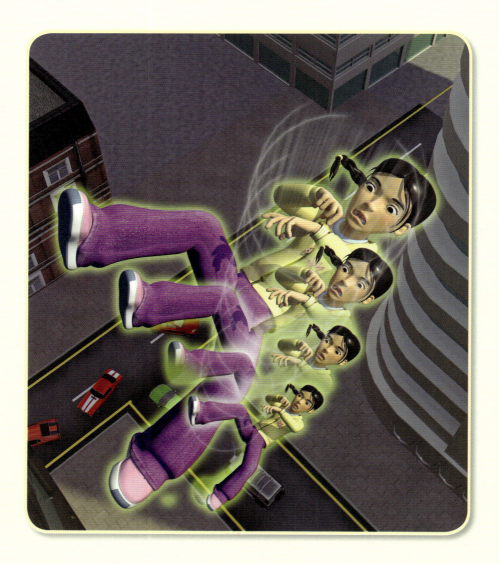

The smaller she became, the more she slowed.
But she did not stop falling. She tumbled over and
over in the air.

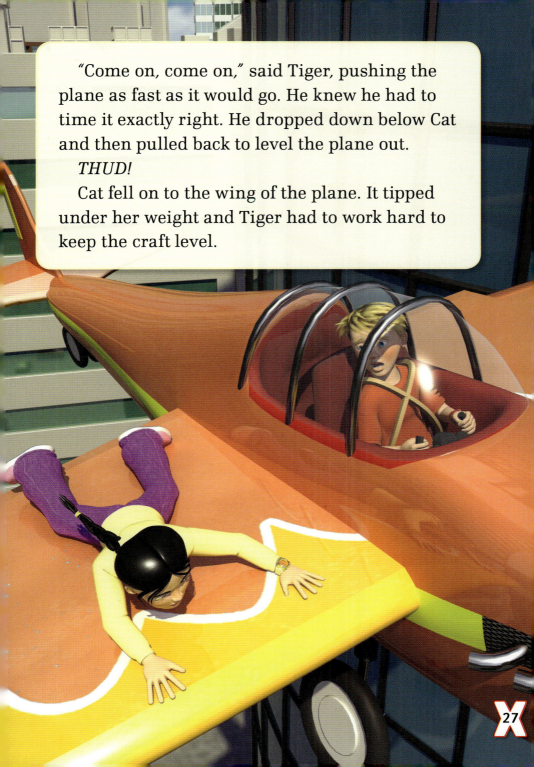

"Come on, come on," said Tiger, pushing the plane as fast as it would go. He knew he had to time it exactly right. He dropped down below Cat and then pulled back to level the plane out.

THUD!

Cat fell on to the wing of the plane. It tipped under her weight and Tiger had to work hard to keep the craft level.

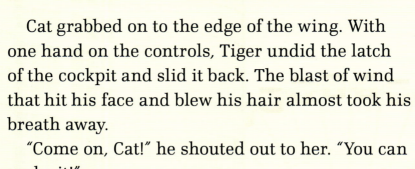

Cat grabbed on to the edge of the wing. With one hand on the controls, Tiger undid the latch of the cockpit and slid it back. The blast of wind that hit his face and blew his hair almost took his breath away.

"Come on, Cat!" he shouted out to her. "You can make it!"

Tiger stretched out his hand. Cat reached out and grabbed it, and Tiger pulled her inside. She was safe.

"Nice of you to drop in," joked Tiger.

"Tiger, don't make me laugh – it hurts!" Cat said, still shaking from her ordeal.

"You, OK?"

"Just a bruise. I'll be fine," she said. "Thank you, Tiger."

"No problem –"

They didn't have time to relax. The X-bot had suddenly realized that Cat had escaped. It let out a piercing scream.

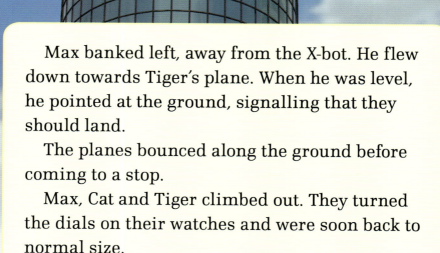

Max banked left, away from the X-bot. He flew down towards Tiger's plane. When he was level, he pointed at the ground, signalling that they should land.

The planes bounced along the ground before coming to a stop.

Max, Cat and Tiger climbed out. They turned the dials on their watches and were soon back to normal size.

Chapter 5 - Return of Robo-Rex

Behind them, the X-bot screamed again. It was making its way back down the side of the NICE building.

"I vote we get out of here," said Cat shakily. She did not fancy another ride with the metal monster.

"Me too," said Tiger.

"Hang on," said Max, "where's Ant?"

"Over here!" called out a voice. Ant was standing by Robo-Rex. "I think we can fix Robo-Rex. Come on, I need your help."

"Let's just leave it. Let's just go!" said Cat.

"Cat," said Max, "we have to try to stop that thing if we can. It's caused enough damage already. Tiger, you want another go at defeating it, don't you?"

"Well ..." said Tiger, unsure.

"Come on!" shouted Ant, waving them over.

Cat had to swallow her fear. "OK."

"Let's do it," said Tiger.

They ran towards Ant. The ground was already beginning to shake as the monster X-bot climbed down.

Ant had noticed that one of Robo-Rex's batteries had fallen out. He pointed to where the cover had come away.

"I don't think it's broken at all," he said. "Quick. Give me a hand!"

They all heaved and shoved, pushing the battery back in place. Ant clicked on the cover.

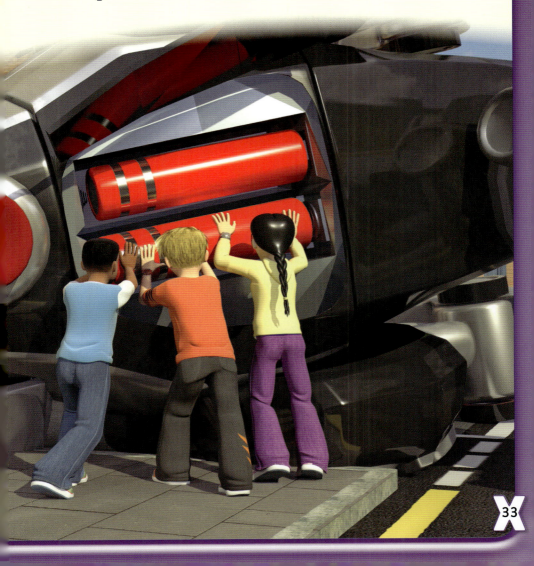

As soon as they had finished, Tiger pulled the remote out of his pocket. He pressed a button and Robo-Rex's eyes lit up.

"Yes!" shouted Tiger. He made the toy clamber to its feet.

Robo-Rex looked a little dizzy. It shook its great head twice. But finally it stood steady, high above them, and let out a fearsome roar.

Back on the ground, the monster X-bot advanced slowly forward.

Cat was not watching – she had noticed a black van at the end of the street. It was the same van she had seen earlier in the day. Then she saw a hand reaching out through the window. It was holding a remote control ... and it was pointing right at the giant X-bot!

Cat crept as quietly as she could towards the van and edged slowly along the side. She peeked into the wing mirror and saw a face she recognized.

"Dr X!" she whispered.

Cat tiptoed backwards, and when she was a safe distance away she ran back to the others.

"Tiger," she said, pointing. "Send Robo-Rex towards that van over there."

"Err, in case you hadn't noticed, we have a giant X-bot about to attack us!" he said.

"What's going on, Cat?" asked Max urgently. "The X-bot will be here any second!"

"There's no time to explain!" said Cat.

Tiger was about to argue but he could see by Cat's face that she had a good reason. He started moving the controls, and Robo-Rex jerked round.

The X-bot bellowed in rage. Tiger tried to ignore it. He moved the controls again and Robo-Rex stomped towards the van.

"Now what?" said Tiger.

"Pick it up," said Cat.

Robo-Rex bent down and picked up the van, its jaws crumpling the sides as if it were made of cardboard.

"Arrggghhhh!" came a cry from the van. "Stop!"

"Dr X!" shouted Max, Ant and Tiger.

"Put me down or I'll –"

"You'll what?" said Tiger, fiddling with the controls.

Robo-Rex shook the van even harder.

"Arrggghhhh!" shouted Dr X again. He dropped his remote control. It landed with a clunk on the ground and Cat bent down to pick it up.

"Thanks very much," said Cat, with a grin.

"Put me down!" yelled Dr X.

"Yeah! Put us down!" yelled his henchmen, Plug and Socket.

Their faces all appeared at the van window.

"You heard the man," said Max, nodding to Tiger.

Tiger grinned and moved the controls. Robo-Rex dropped the van, which fell to the ground with a great crash.

Dr X, Plug and Socket staggered from the battered van, groaning.

"Don't hurt us!" said Plug.

"We give in!" shouted Socket, waving a white hanky.

"No we don't!" hissed Dr X. "What kind of evil villain gives in to a bunch of kids?"

Cat tossed Dr X's remote to Tiger. Tiger grinned. He tucked the Robo-Rex remote into his pocket and pushed the controls of Dr X's controller. The X-bot stopped in its tracks and then turned to face Dr X.

"Careful," said Dr X. "That's a very dangerous piece of machinery. It isn't a toy!"

Tiger flicked the controls and the X-bot's eyes glowed menacingly. It lifted one of its feet up and smashed it down towards Dr X and his men. They only just managed to leap out of the way in time as the monster X-bot's claw smashed the pavement.

"Steady on, Tiger," said Max.

"It's not me ... the controls aren't working," said Tiger, with a frown.

"It must have got damaged when it fell from the van," said Ant. "We're back where we started."

Tiger dropped the X-bot's remote and took out Robo-Rex's controls. "Here we go again!" said Tiger. With that, he made Robo-Rex charge at the X-bot.

The two giants clashed once more. Tiger and Robo-Rex fought bravely, but Tiger felt the controls begin to slow. "Uh, oh, I think the batteries really are running out this time."

Suddenly Ant ran forwards.

"Where are you going?" yelled Max.

"Stay there!" shouted Ant to the others. He ran towards the fighting giants, dodging the stomping feet of Robo-Rex.

"Ant! Get out the way!" screamed Tiger.

But Ant didn't listen. Instead he ran up to the monster X-bot and grabbed its cold, shiny leg.

Quick as a flash, Ant turned the dial on his watch.
He pushed the X and ...

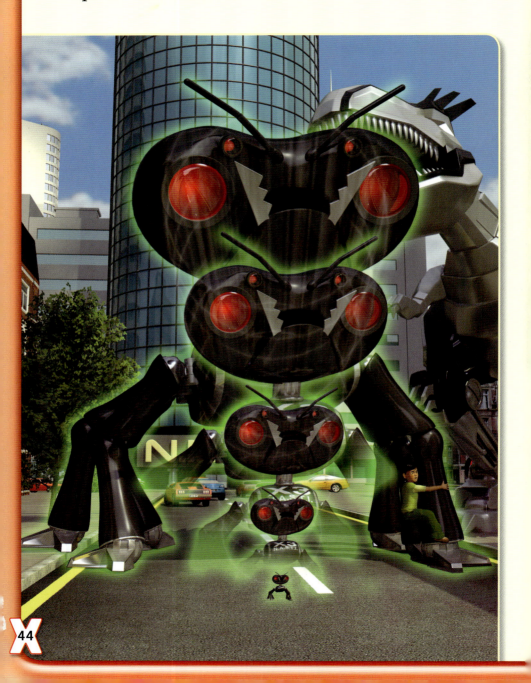

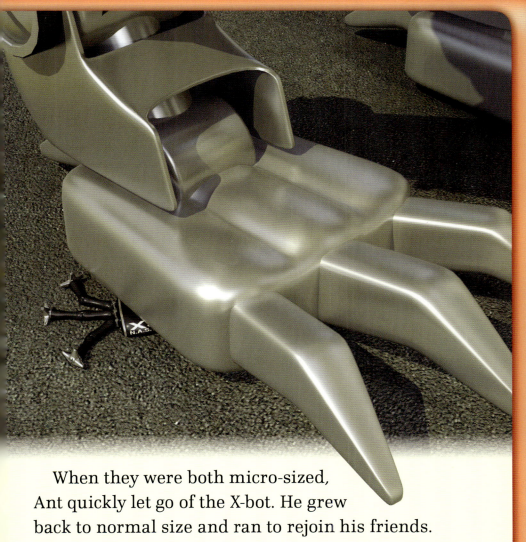

When they were both micro-sized,
Ant quickly let go of the X-bot. He grew
back to normal size and ran to rejoin his friends.

The tiny X-bot ran around looking confused. Tiger
brought one of Robo-Rex's giant feet down on the X-bot,
squashing it flat. Then the glow faded from Robo-Rex's
eyes as the batteries finally died.

The children looked round. Dr X, Plug and Socket
were nowhere to be seen.

A siren wailed in the distance.

"It's the police," said Max. He pointed at Robo-Rex. "Perhaps we ought to do something about him as well. If the police arrive and Robo-Rex is still a giant ... well, it will take a lot of explaining!"

Tiger sighed. He liked the idea of having a giant remote-controlled Robo-Rex as a toy. Then again, it would hardly fit in his house, let alone his toy box! He stood on Robo-Rex's foot. He turned the dial on his watch. "You're still the best, whatever size you are."

GREENVILLE NEWS

Robot Rampage or Robot Hoax?

Cinema goers were caught up in an amazing spectacle today when their film *Robot Rampage* was interrupted – by a "real" monster robot!

It appears that a publicity stunt for the opening of the film got out of hand. The company behind the film were quick to deny their involvement.

Police are trying to trace the owners of a black van that was damaged in the incident but so far they have had no success.

One woman watching the film reported seeing a 'giant black robot with red eyes' but the police think that the van must have reversed through the wall – it was the red brake lights the audience saw.

"The brain is a curious thing," said an expert. "Because she was watching an exciting film about robots, her eyes were tricked into seeing a robot, when, of course, it was just the back end of a van."

Find out more ...

For another exciting adventure, read *Journey to Mars*.

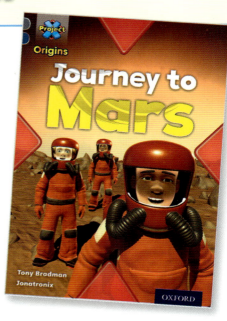

To go **Behind the Scenes** of real film stunts, read *Spectacular Film Stunts*.

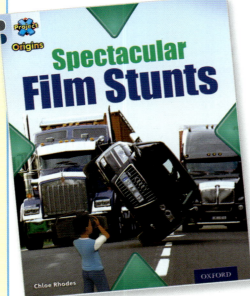